GARFIELD

Classics

Volume Two

MY SECOND CLASSIC COLLECTION
CONTAINS:

ADMIT IT, ODIE'S OK!

TWO'S COMPANY

WHAT'S COOKING?

JiM DAViS   ℛ

© 1998 PAWS INCORPORATED
(www.garfield.com)

All rights reserved.
"GARFIELD" and the GARFIELD characters
are registered and unregistered trademarks
of Paws, Incorporated.

First published by Ravette Publishing 1998
Reprinted 1999, 2000, 2001

This book is sold subject to the condition that
it shall not, by way of trade or otherwise, be
lent, resold, hired out or otherwise circulated
without the publisher's prior consent in any
form of binding or cover other than that in
which it is published and without a similar
condition including this condition being
imposed on the subsequent purchaser.

Printed and bound in Great Britain
for Ravette Publishing Limited,
Unit 3, Tristar Centre,
Star Road, Partridge Green,
West Sussex RH13 8RA
by Cox & Wyman Ltd, Reading, Berkshire

ISBN 1 85304 971 9

Garfield
Admit it, Odie's O.K.!

JIM DAVIS

JIM DAViS   9-18

© 1982 United Feature Syndicate, Inc.

© 1982 United Feature Syndicate, Inc.

© 1982 United Feature Syndicate, Inc.

© 1982 United Feature Syndicate, Inc.

JIM DAVIS 9-14

© 1982 United Feature Syndicate, Inc.

BARK

© 1982 United Feature Syndicate, Inc.

ARRRGH!

VERY FUNNY, ODIE. NOW GET YOUR FACE OFF THE WINDOW

© 1982 United Feature Syndicate, Inc.

© 1982 United Feature Syndicate, Inc.

GETTING OUT OF THIS TREE WILL BE SIMPLER THAN I THOUGHT

JIM DAVIS

6-12

© 1982 United Feature Syndicate, Inc

JIM DAVIS 5-18

CHUG!

YOU'RE A REAL BEAR UNTIL YOU'VE HAD YOUR FIRST CUP OF COFFEE, AREN'T YOU?

AND THEN I'M THE SWEETEST SO-AND-SO AROUND

© 1982 United Feature Syndicate, Inc.

© 1982 United Feature Syndicate, Inc.

7-21

© 1982 United Feature Syndicate, Inc.

© 1982 United Feature Syndicate, Inc.

DON'T YOU DARE WALK
ACROSS THE TABLE WITH
THOSE MUDDY FEET

© 1982 United Feature Syndicate, Inc.

9-2

© 1982 United Feature Syndicate, Inc.

© 1982 United Feature Syndicate, Inc.

© 1982 United Feature Syndicate, Inc.

I GOTTA FIX THAT VERTICAL HOLD

© 1982 United Feature Syndicate, Inc.

WAH-CHOO!

WAH-CHOO!

© 1982 United Feature Syndicate, Inc.

6-28

IT'S TIME YOU GO ON ANOTHER DIET, GARFIELD

© 1982 United Feature Syndicate, Inc.

© 1982 United Feature Syndicate, Inc.

© 1982 United Feature Syndicate, Inc.

JIM DAVIS

11-5

© 1981 United Feature Syndicate, Inc.

© 1981 United Feature Syndicate, Inc.

JIM DAVIS

© 1981 United Feature Syndicate, Inc.

6-14

© 1982 United Feature Syndicate, Inc.

© 1982 United Feature Syndicate, Inc.

GARFIELD'S LAW:
CATS ARE INDEPENDENT.
CATS ARE LONERS...

THEY ARE UNDERFOOT
ONLY WHEN YOU'RE
CARRYING GROCERIES

SORRY
ABOUT
THAT

9-21 · JIM DAVIS

SPLAT

A VERY SHORT
BUT NEAT
RAIN SHOWER

© 1982 United Feature Syndicate, Inc.

© 1982 United Feature Syndicate, Inc.

HELLO. I'M NERMAL, THE WORLD'S CUTEST KITTEN, HERE TO DO CUTE KITTEN THINGS IN ORDER TO CHARM THE PANTS OFF YOUR OWNER AND POINT OUT HOW UNCUTE YOU ARE

I HATE MONDAY

© 1982 United Feature Syndicate, Inc.

© 1982 United Feature Syndicate, Inc.

© 1982 United Feature Syndicate, Inc.

GARFIELD HAS THE UNIQUE ABILITY TO HEAR A CAN OPENER FROM ANYWHERE IN THE HOUSE

RRRRRRR

JIM DAVIS   3-18

WHA...

© 1982 United Feature Syndicate, Inc.

© 1982 United Feature Syndicate, Inc.

Garfield
Two's Company

JIM DAVIS

© 1983 United Feature Syndicate, Inc.

© 1983 United Feature Syndicate, Inc.   9-26

© 1983 United Feature Syndicate, Inc.

© 1983 United Feature Syndicate, Inc.

JIM DAVIS 9-30

© 1983 United Feature Syndicate, Inc.

© 1982 United Feature Syndicate, Inc.

© 1982 United Feature Syndicate, Inc.

© 1982 United Feature Syndicate, Inc.

© 1982 United Feature Syndicate, Inc.

12-2

© 1982 United Feature Syndicate, Inc.

JON WILL BE CHECKING THIS TRAP SOON

© 1982 United Feature Syndicate, Inc.

MY BUNNY SLIPPERS?

THEY LIKE TO ROAM AT NIGHT

12-4

JIM DAVIS

© 1963 United Feature Syndicate, Inc.

THE CAPTAIN HAS ADVISED THAT THE "FASTEN SEAT BELT" SIGN BE OBSERVED IN CASE SOME SLIGHT AIR TURBULENCE IS ENCOUNTERED

THIS IS GOING TO UPSET YOU, GARFIELD...

JIM DAVIS 4·23

BECAUSE I KNOW YOU'VE HAD A GREAT TIME

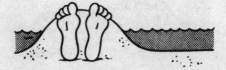

© 1983 United Feature Syndicate, Inc.

BUT IT'S TIME WE THINK ABOUT GOING HOME

I DIDN'T KNOW YOU LIKE TO DANCE, GARFIELD

WHAT ARE YOU TALKING ABOUT?

I WAS SCRATCHING MY BACK WITH YOUR TOOTHBRUSH

© 1982 United Feature Syndicate, Inc.

© 1983 United Feature Syndicate, Inc.

NICE TRY, GARFIELD, BUT I DON'T BUY YOUR STUPID WATERMELON DISGUISE

© 1983 United Feature Syndicate, Inc.

RATA TATTA TATTA TAT

HEY, GARFIELD, WHEN WAS THE LAST TIME YOU SAW MY PET FROG, HERBIE?

SNAK!

AT LUNCH

© 1983 United Feature Syndicate, Inc.

© 1983 United Feature Syndicate, Inc.

© 1983 United Feature Syndicate, Inc.

© 1983 United Feature Syndicate, Inc.

STOP PLAYING
WITH YOUR FOOD,
GARFIELD

© 1983 United Feature Syndicate, Inc.

I'M NOT.
IT DRIED OUT
WHILE MY
FACE WAS
IN IT

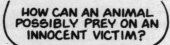

GOOD! THEY SHOT THE LION!

JIM DAVIS

WHAT DO YOU THINK OF THOSE APPLES, GARFIELD?

BIG DEAL

© 1983 United Feature Syndicate, Inc.

2-18

AT THE GUN IT WAS VILLAGERS: 1, LION: 42

© 1983 United Feature Syndicate, Inc.

© 1963 United Feature Syndicate, Inc.

© 1983 United Feature Syndicate, Inc.

YOU'VE BEEN READING "ALICE IN WONDERLAND" AGAIN, HAVEN'T YOU?

YOU MUS BE PSYCHI

8-3   JIM DAV??

7-19

© 1983 United Feature Syndicate, Inc.

Garfield

What's Cooking?

JIM DAVIS

1-22

© 1983 United Feature Syndicate, Inc.

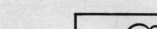

WINDOWS ARE GREAT. THEY OFFER A FRONT ROW SEAT TO LIFE'S PASSING PARADE

JIM DAVIS   12-7

© 1982 United Feature Syndicate, Inc.

THUD!

THEY ARE ALSO GOOD FOR A YUK OR TWO

© 1983 United Feature Syndicate, Inc.

© 1982 United Feature Syndicate, Inc.

© 1982 United Feature Syndicate, Inc.

© 1982 United Feature Syndicate, Inc.

© 1983 United Feature Syndicate, Inc.

© 1983 United Feature Syndicate, Inc.

© 1983 United Feature Syndicate, Inc.

© 1983 United Feature Syndicate, Inc.

© 1983 United Feature Syndicate, Inc.

© 1983 United Feature Syndicate, Inc.

© 1983 United Feature Syndicate, Inc.

HOP
HOP
HOP

JIM DAVIS

9-23

HOP

© 1983 United Feature Syndicate, Inc.

LEG WARMERS

© 1963 United Feature Syndicate, Inc.

© 1983 United Feature Syndicate, Inc.

11-1   JIM DAVIS

I'M TAKING THIS STEAK AND THERE'S NOTHING YOU CAN DO ABOUT IT, CHIPMUNK CHEEKS

© 1963 United Feature Syndicate, Inc.

I'VE ALWAYS ENCOURAGED GARFIELD TO BE ASSERTIVE. BUT I BELIEVE HE'S CROSSED THE FINE LINE TO OBNOXIOUS

© 1983 United Feature Syndicate, Inc.

© 1983 United Feature Syndicate, Inc.